The Sliding Glass Door
~ My Journey ~

K. Jill Jewell Barr

PublishAmerica
Baltimore

First printing

At the specific preference of the author, PublishAmerica allowed this work to remain exactly as the author intended, verbatim, without editorial input.

ISBN: 1-4137-7705-8
PUBLISHED BY PUBLISHAMERICA, LLLP
www.publishamerica.com
Baltimore

Printed in the United States of America

This book is dedicated to my children,
Tyler and Braeden.
They are the absolute greatest loves of my life.

~ *Acknowledgements* ~

A special thanks to my parents for raising me in such a loving and supportive home and for your continued support through the years.

A special thanks to Diana, Fran and Ashley for each of your friendship, guidance and constructive criticism over the years.

Thanks to the Ghosts of My Past for being the Stepping Stones that led me along My Journey and a special thanks to the one whose friendship I hold dear and who inspired some very significant healing words.

And lastly, a very special thanks to my Painter, Hugh, for not only helping in the design of the book cover, but for the fairy tale of love and for showing me more love than I ever dreamt possible.

> "She wants to sleep in peace
> And be held in strong arms.
> She only wants the fairy tale of love,
> Of finding love and love finding her."

Gratitude and Love to All,

~Jill

~ *Contents* ~

Until another time...
And in another place...
Perhaps one day soon...
We will meet face to face...

The Fairy Tale

Once upon a time
There lived a girl
Who searched and searched
All over the world

For a love so right
And a touch so sweet
All embodied in a boy
She hoped to soon meet.

Out of the blue
That day soon came.
She met her prince
And was never the same.

He was kind and gentle
With a love so pure.
It was love at first sight
That will ever endure.

She was under his spell
And in a state of bliss
All from the sweet taste
Of one perfect kiss.

She was his to love.
Their love was foretold,
Pledged to each other
Until they grow old.

A great love was found.
Their hearts were captured.
They were destined to live
Happily forever after.

Still Waters

The still waters are ever so calm
As I reflect back on my life
And realize that even the smallest
Of ripples is significant.

This Pain Inside of Me

Some things in life
Happen for no reason.
People come and they go
Just like the change of a season.

To love beyond understanding
Is something I've never known.
To not feel and allow myself not to love
Reminds me I am all alone.

By choice or my fate,
Regardless of the cause,
I am alone within myself
Surrounded by each of my flaws.

I hurt beyond reason,
A pain down deep inside.
I care because of my desires.
My hurt I can no longer abide.

I pretend I do not hurt.
I sit and allow the pain to be.
I am convinced all are fooled
But the biggest fool is me.

I've hidden all my wounds
From all the world to see.
I've kept them buried
Deep down inside of me.

That is where they've been
For time so very long.
Pain alone can't hurt me.
It serves to make me strong.

I've loved and I've lost,
The story of my life.
I've lived hard years
And was mistreated as a wife.

My pain stems from this.
I succumb and I secede,
A hurt beyond imagine
And in the end lost sight of me.

I know I'm here somewhere.
I've just got to be.
I need to just let go
Of this pain inside of me.

How do I begin?
And just where do I start?
How can I repair
All the breaks in my heart?

I'm afraid to love
Or love's afraid of me.
I can't take the pain.
I guess that's the key.

The key to all reason,
To understand my despair
And realize most of all
That sometimes life is unfair.

I was meant to love
In due time with certainty.
But just how do I heal
All this pain inside of me?

It hurts just to breathe,
To feel the pressure on my heart,
To know it's weighted down
And has been torn apart.

I haven't the answer,
Nor do I know what's right,
But I've come to discover that
With love I'm quick to seek flight.

To flee away and run
And try not to look back,
That is my defense,
The mode of my attack.

I can't seem to love
Nor let love stay and be.
I guess it's all because
Of this pain inside of me

I do want to love
In due time with certainty.
I just have to be patient
And when right, love will find me.

My burdens I need to lay down
And let the hurt be set free,
So that I no longer have
This pain inside of me.

Untitled

The pieces of my heart
Are scattered all about.
I'm left to sit and think,
To wonder and to doubt.
Will there ever be someone for me
Whom I can call my own?
Someone to build a life with
And make a happy home?

The Gypsy

She was part girl, part woman,
Part gypsy, part witch.
She lived for love
And love lived for her.

She spent her days in boredom
And her nights in restless sleep.
She tossed and turned
Afraid of what the morning held for her.

She had given her heart freely in the past
And the love she gave was to be cherished.
Her outward beauty was nothing
Compared to the beauty within her.

Many were quick to take the love she gave,
But so few were willing to give her love in return.
Her heart had been broken time and time again.
She sealed up her heart and kept the love inside of her.

More than anything she wanted to find love
And for love to find her.
She wanted to find the love that matched hers.
She wanted to find the one meant only for her.

At last she found who she hoped was the one
Who made her feel with all of her being.
She wanted to take a chance at love again
And give everything she held inside of her.

But she was afraid,
Afraid at losing that feeling again,
Afraid of being denied love again,
Afraid to let the love out from within her.

As mysterious as she appeared on the outside,
She was really nothing more than an open book.
And she carried her heart on her sleeve,
Desperately looking for the one to have it and hold her.

The gypsy within her
Calmed the fears of the girl.
And the witch in her
Added to the mystery of the woman in her.

She roamed and roamed
Restless and discontented
Searching for the soul
That completed all of her.

Much like a gypsy,
Never content to leave her heart
In one place for very long,
Afraid of losing the person inside of her.

The hurt girl within her
Kept her afraid to feel.
For when she did allow the feelings to flow,
They were always torn from her.

Her heart could take no more,
No more love lost,
No more denied feelings,
No more pain from inside of her.

The gypsy has fallen.
The woman is in pain,
Pain felt from impending heartbreak
For she is feeling love within her.

Her chest is heavy,
With each beat of her heart,
And each breath she does take,
Full of love ready to escape from her.

Uncertainty and self-doubt,
Not knowing if her love will be returned,
Not knowing if she will be deemed worthy
Of him accepting the love within her.

She wants to sleep in peace
And be held in strong arms.
She only wants the fairy tale of love,
Of finding love and love finding her.

Echo

Her life was like an echo
Destined to repeat again and again.
Each time she found love
It managed to come to an end.

Her eyes hid years and years of abuse.
Her heart contained so many breaks.
Something was missing from her life
That she hoped could soothe some of her aches.

The echo of each break of her heart
Could be heard from distances great.
She longed for peace and love
And to be held and to be safe.

Her wants were few
But her needs were vast.
She deserved to find love
And for that love to last.

Each pounding beat of her heart
Echoed the hurt it contained,
As she searched and searched
For that perfect love to be gained.

The echo of her life
Was with her each step of the way.
Its repetition constant and reminiscent
Of the morning shedding light to a new day.

Wounded Bird

Like a wounded bird,
She couldn't leave the ground.
Her wings were clipped
And her heart was bound.

Many years ago
She was frightened and alone.
Her life was dark.
The sun never shown.

Her worth was cheapened.
Her pride had gone away.
Her spirit had died
But the price, she did pay.

Life's lessons were hard.
She's grown through the years.
She's learned from her past
And she's conquered her fears.

Her soul was wounded,
As were her body and heart.
Her feelings were hurt
Almost from the start.

Yet she endured and she sustained.
She put up the good fight.
She tolerated so much
That she knew wasn't right.

With clipped wings and all,
No flight was in her path.
Her options were few
But she escaped at last.

This wounded bird
Has found skies of blue.
She's soaring so high
With a love fresh and new.

No one can erase
The memories of her past.
She will ever be wounded.
Some wounds always last.

Her pain inside
Has no boundary, no end.
But the love she's found
Has her soaring again.

Her wings are no longer clipped.
Her heart is no longer bound.
For the love of her life,
She has finally found.

Me

When you look at me
I want you to see me,
Not some adornment on the outside
But my inner beauty.

I want to feel your gaze
As you look into my soul,
And when you see what's in my heart
And know it's yours to hold.

I want you to see me
And know without a doubt,
That you want the love I have
And know you can't live without.

I want your understanding
Of my very painful past.
I want you to see me
And know you'll be the last.

I want you to know me
And all my childhood years.
I want your understanding
When I shed my tears.

I'm so full of passion
And very sensitive, that's me.
I'm also very caring
And cursed emotionally.

I feel the pain of others
Because of what I have felt
In my quest for love
With what I've been dealt.

When you look into my eyes
I want you to see what's there,
Beyond my blue eyes
And my golden blond hair.

When you look at me
I want you to see me,
The person that I am inside
In all my spectacular glory.

Him

A true gentleman he is
Sweet touch, nice smile.
I hope to be in his presence
For a very long while.

I look forward to the days ahead
Filled with his zest and his charm
And spending long nights
Being held in his arms.

Sliding Glass Door

I woke up with a smile on my face
Left over from the night before
That was put there in place
As I walked through your sliding glass door.

After the storms I have weathered,
You are a bright sunny day.
And our first time together,
I will carry with me always.

You touched and embraced me
And held me so tight.
Your arms protected me
And made everything right.

I felt like I belonged
And my journey was through.
I'd finally found some peace
And I found it with you.

I felt protected and needed.
My fears you've helped calm.
You gave me something in return.
We were together as one.

My heart is racing,
My emotions on high.
I'm feeling things
I've not felt for a while.

You put a smile on my face
And there's love in my heart
That's ready to escape
But it needs a head start.

I'm not very patient
And my trust levels are low,
But I trust you completely.
My heart, you control.

I fell asleep last night with a smile on my face
Left over from the hours before
That was put there by you
When I walked through your sliding glass door.

I Cried in Your Arms

I cried in your arms
From the shear joy
Of feeling something
I've searched for forever.

I cried in your arms
Not from hurt or pain
But because I felt something
Pure and wonderful.

I cried in your arms
Because what has been
Locked away inside of me
For so long, seeped out.

I cried in your arms
Because I'd found my place.
I'd found what I needed
And what I've wanted.

I cried in your arms
Because you set
The pain inside of me
Free.

About Tonight

About tonight
Plans not set in stone
Spending time together
Is all that is known.

You and me
Draped in each other
Igniting with passion
Becoming lovers.

In another time
And in another place
Connected by wires
Each an unknown face.

We found the place
We found the time
We finally did meet
A perfect rhyme.

Day By Day With You

More and more better
Day by day with you,
Each day with you in it
Is quite terrific for me too.

A breath of fresh air,
A warm breeze on a summer day,
You bring passion to my life
Like the heat from the sun's ray.

My life has changed so much
Over such a short span of time.
I have been lifted so high.
You put meaning to my rhyme.

More and more better
Day by day with you,
You have made my life better
Just by being you.

A Smile on My Face

I'm quite smitten with you
I must admit.
You add joy to my days
And put smiles on my face.

I've been content most of my life,
But not happy.
My smiles were few and far between.
You definitely make my heart sing.

You're thoughtful and caring
And very sincere.
I'm not used to this.
You're a come true wish.

Just a small thought of you
Makes me sigh.
It makes my heart race
And puts a smile on my face.

The Princess

She lived in a glass house
Frozen in time.
He melted her heart
And mesmerized her mind.

She'd found her prince in shining armor
With a love so sweet and right.
She found love in those arms
That held her so close and tight.

She'd wandered through life
With a purpose unknown.
She's reached the end of her journey
And found a place to call home.

His arms hold all the warmth,
Protective and strong.
His eyes hold her heart.
It sings such a sweet song.

Beautiful music together
Is what they make.
And when they make love,
Their breath it does take.

The fairy tale of love
Is what she has found.
To love and be loved
Makes the world go 'round.

The Princess has shed her last tear.
Her heart has found its owner.
All the past breaks have been mended
With the love he has shown her.

So much to look forward to,
So many journeys to take,
But this time they're together,
Each other to not forsake.

Passion and feeling,
This great love they are due.
With the days ahead,
Together just the two.

The glass house has been shattered.
Its doors opened wide.
Her heart has been released
Of all the pain it held inside.

The Painter and The Poet

The Painter and the Poet
Met one autumn day.
With a slight nip in the air,
Their breath was taken away.

This meeting was life changing.
Each now had a face to a name.
An instant connection was formed.
Now neither will ever be the same.

From the sweetest kiss on her cheek,
The Poet was knocked off her stance.
Her heart and eyes were opened
And a great love she wanted to chance.

Full of expression and vision,
She with her words, he with his brush,
They are magical together
And are creating so much.

She with her pen and her paper,
Bares all of her heart.
He with his paint and his canvas,
Creates a lasting mark.

The Painter and the Poet,
Two peas in a pod,
Were destined to find each other.
It was fated by God.

Ghosts of The Past

The ghosts of my past
Haunt my future and my present.
My insecurities are so vast.
My weariness is spent.

Past memories are filled
With heartache and love lost.
They cloud my mind now.
In the confusion, I've been caught.

The ghosts of your past
Haunt me and what I feel.
I'm overpowered with doubt
And want what I feel to be real.

Thoughts of those
That have fallen before me
And found warmth in your arms
Blinds me so very fiercely.

The ghosts of the past
Make it difficult for me to breathe.
I so want and need
My insecurities to be set free.

The love and desire in my heart
Is deemed only for one
Who is loyal and trusting
And will do me no wrong.

The ghosts of our past
Can be found in our minds.
Those ghosts of the past
Need to be left behind.

I'm too weary to compete
With a faded memory.
The ghosts of the past
Won't come between you and me.

We can learn from those
Whose love did not last.
They can teach us so much,
The ghosts of the past.

My Sweet Prince

Goodnight my sweet prince
Oh how I hate to see you go
As our day comes to an end
And I start to miss you so.

I wish you could climb inside my heart
And see how much I feel for you.
I wish you could just get a glimpse
And take in a bird's eye view.

My days revolve around you
And my nights are bound with dreams of more tomorrows,
Dreams of you and how you make me smile.
You have effortlessly erased all my sorrows.

I've grown accustomed to your presence,
Your smile, your kiss and your feel.
You have become my want and my need.
My sweet prince, you are so very real.

As you close your eyes
And drift off to your night's sleep,
Know I am with you as you rest
And I am yours to keep.

Writer of Words

I am a writer of words
And a thinker of thoughts.
Invading my mind with cruelty
Is easily done and I pay the cost.

I've searched the world over
And finally found my place.
Some evil outside interest
Will not turn my face.

I will stand strong and proud
And fight for what is true.
I'll not let mistrust
Come between me and you.

I love you too much
To just turn and flee.
With you, beside you
Is where you'll find me.

I usually run when darkness looms close,
Lurking and hurting all in its path,
But not this time, no.
I'll be firmly planted in its aftermath.

It'll take a lot more
To turn this good to mere bad.
Not a man nor a woman
Can make me feel sad.

My words and my thoughts
Are my own enemies.
A third party is not needed
To find my insecurities.

I love so much it hurts
When my heart is alone
Sheltered and secluded
From the love it's been shown.

My heart is so big
It feels so much more
Than anyone could imagine
With a love so pure.

Its flaws are quite visible
When you chance a deep look.
You'll see the pain it has suffered
Hidden in each and every nook.

This writer of words
And this thinker of thoughts
Is her own worst critic
When finding her faults.

I'm not perfect I know
Nor do I claim to be,
But search the world over
And you'll find no other like me.

Like This

I've loved before or so I thought
But I've never felt quite like this.
It is indescribable in a wonderful way
Like I've been blessed with a gift.

And I do feel greatly blessed
Like someone is watching over me
And granting me wishes from long ago
When I wished on each star I would see.

I've always been a giver, not a taker
And have shown more love than was returned.
I just blindly opened up my heart
And in the end my heart got burned.

I've given more of myself in the past
And not held back like I probably should.
I've allowed my heart to be played
As if it were not made of feelings but of wood.

I look for the good in those I meet,
Those I want to chance a friendship with.
And I have felt love before, a time or two,
But not like yours and not like this.

You have left me wanting and yearning
For so much more than I deserve.
And my heart that was stuck in the past
Is now peddling ahead and is no longer in reverse.

I love loving you, more than you'll know.
My lips are reserved only for your kiss.
I've loved before, a time or two,
But nothing comes close to feeling like this.

His Words

"You're beautiful and sweet and I Love You!"
Are but just a few of the things he's said.
"I enjoy every aspect of you from all angles",
Makes me melt and swells my head.

I'm not accustomed to such romance
Or words so tender and sweet.
He is the broom that has swept me
Over and off of my feet.

He's thrown caution to the wind
And has stepped into the sun with me.
Our days are ever filled with laughter
And our nights serve only to please.

He is the Painter to my Poet.
His words are set to my rhyme.
He is all the inspiration that I need
To carry me through all of time.

My face has never smiled so much
Nor have kisses been ever so sweet.
I am so fully blessed and can't imagine
Where I'd be if never we did meet.

I've never felt quite like this
Of that you can be sure.
I surely do hope this fairy tale love
Will ever and always endure.

His love brings peace to my soul.
His heart is like a sliding glass door.
Together they embrace me completely,
Always willing to give so much more.

His words are more precious to me than gold.
His touch is much softer than silk.
The depth and love I see in his eyes
Makes me puddle up and wilt.

And oh how he makes me sigh
When he loves me ever so tender.
I am relaxed as I can be from loving him,
As the heat we ignite is left to cinder.

He is the Prince to my Princess.
He is the right to all my wrongs.
His words are my saving grace
And with him is where I'll always belong.

Your Girl

The onset of the rest of my life began
That beautiful day that you entered my world.
You added your wonderful spirit to my life
When you named me as your girl.

I am completely yours and yours alone.
No one and no thing can turn me from you.
You are what I have waited to find.
Your girl is stuck to you like glue.

The expectations that I had for love
Compare nothing at all to this.
I'm so happy and content with you
And long only for your kiss.

I love being all tangled up with you
With you all wrapped up in me.
A love this great and a feeling this strong
Is almost too good to believe.

I am your girl for now and evermore.
No other man can ever claim me as his.
You're all that I want out of life.
You are my only desire and wish.

My heart is filled with love for you,
For you and you alone.
Your girl has found her heart's desire.
It's with you that she's found home.

When I Am Not Near

I hope you feel my breath
Whisper softly in your ear
And can feel my presence
Even when I am not near.

All the words I write
And the thoughts I think
Are but a mere sample
Of a never ending link.

Apart, not together,
With you there and me here,
I hope you sense my love
Even when I am not near.

I'm touched and very blessed
To have you in my life.
I've found that connection
That matches mine in strife.

You are my everything,
My love, my life, my dear.
I long always to be with you
Even when I am not near.

I love you never meant so much.
This much feeling I've never quite felt.
You've thawed out my heart
And made all its iciness melt.

My love ever kind and true
Will always and ever be here.
My heart will always belong to you
Even when I am not near.

My Inner Feelings

I have so much inside
That I want to share with you.
My feelings and emotions,
They are ever so true.

I don't think you comprehend
Or fully understand
Just what it is I feel for you
Or what you hold in your hand.

You hold all of me,
My soul and my heart.
My body is yours too.
I hurt when we are apart.

The depth of what I feel
Is more than words could say.
I can't imagine what I would do
If ever you went away.

I closed up my heart for a time
And allowed myself not to feel.
I shielded myself from further pain
But the plug in my heart did not seal.

My inner feelings escaped.
Nothing could stop what I felt for you.
The lock on my heart opened up
And I fell in love so deep and true.

Thirty-One Days

A month ago today
Your lips lightly grazed my face.
My life as it was
Had forever been erased.

Happiness has found me
And graced my face with smiles.
Your love has embraced my heart
And left its mark for miles.

For thirty-one days
And just as many nights,
I've been blessed with greatness
And raised to new heights.

You've shown me more love
Than I ever had known
With very little effort
And with your heart alone.

I've had thirty-one days
Of not feeling blue.
I've spent a month of my life
Being loved by you.

A Face Unknown

I dreamt of you long before I ever found you.
You haunted my dreams with a face unknown.
I would awake to find you no longer there.
Your presence was very real, yet I was all alone.

I still dream of you when I close my eyes to rest.
Your face is no longer unknown to me.
I have memorized each detail of it.
It is forever etched in my memory.

Loving you is my key and my purpose.
Finding you was my saving grace.
I'd never been happy before,
But with you I've found my place.

A face unknown is what you were to me
In the darkness of night behind my eyes.
In the light of day I searched until I found you
And saw your face and revealed its disguise.

My Senses

The smell of wood burning in the fireplace,
The feel of worn flannel against my skin,
The sight of your sexy eyes and handsome face,
The taste of your sweet kisses on my lips,
And the sound of your voice each cause my heart to race.

My senses lead me to you.
You are all I want out of life.
There is nothing on earth I'd rather do
Than to spend my days wrapped in your arms
And my nights being loved by you.

Your eyes show more depth than I've ever seen.
Your voice always finds just the right words.
Your taste seeks perfection, nothing in between.
Your touch compares to nothing I've ever felt.
And your senses for me are ever so keen.

My feelings for you are exact and strong.
Your feelings for me are kind and true.
My love for you will last for time so long.
Your love for me is felt deep within my soul.
And you and I together can never be wrong.

Just Holding Your Hand

I don't need diamonds or pearls
To be your girl.
It just takes the touch of your hand
For me to know you're my man.

My heart swims with feelings so very new.
My blood runs warm with thoughts of you.
It's not so difficult to understand.
I'm perfectly content just holding your hand.

My love runs true and deep.
I'm content to be held by you while I sleep.
I long for your sweet embrace,
And look forward to the days we will face.

My love, my life, that's you,
A fresh start, a beginning new.
Your hand in my hand, tender and right.
Your heart with my heart, a fit so tight.

I don't need riches or jewels.
They're merely gold for fools.
I'm content just holding your hand,
Being your girl and you being my man.

Yours

I was yours from the moment
You kissed my cheek.
It was romantic and tender
And ever so sweet.

You changed my life for the better
With one brief kiss.
I'd never imagined
That I would ever feel like this.

I am so enamored by you,
So full of heat and passion.
I've never felt this strong,
In manner or in fashion.

I belong to you
And have found my niche.
I only want you.
You're what makes my heart tick.

Do you get it?
Do you see?
Can you feel this love I have
For you inside of me?

You are my everything
And I cherish you so much.
I never want to take for granted
Your love or your touch.

I am yours.
With you is where I belong.
The love I have for you
Is yours and yours alone.

The Doubt of Shadow

How long 'til you decide
That you don't want me anymore?
When will you change your mind
And go back like you were before?

How much time do we have
Before you realize you were wrong,
And that someone from the past
Is who you've loved all along?

That little thread of doubt
Has been planted in my mind.
The security that I had
Has been left far behind.

I question and I doubt
All that I've come to know.
I'm very much in fear
That you will one day go.

I've given you my all
And everything I have.
You've reached a part of me
And cleared away a path.

I can't fight any more demons,
Those ghosts from your past.
I haven't the strength left in me.
The doubt of shadow has been cast.

I'm frightened and bewildered
With all the emotions that I feel.
I fear that you will vanish
And will turn to dust and not be real.

I'm nothing special.
That's been drilled in my head.
And I know that several can replace me
In your heart and in your bed.

I think too much I know
And let my worries cloud my mind.
I'm trying to be strong
And not let that happen this time.

But it is so hard to do,
To keep my breath from spilling out.
Life without your love and you in it
Is not something I chance to live without.

I'm deeply in love with you.
I can feel it in my bones.
You are it for me.
With any other, I'd still be alone.

I want so much
To live each day with you.
I see a happy life ahead.
Its colors painted a pretty hue.

You're my one and only,
The completion to all of me.
The doubt of shadow
I know need not be.

A Past Memory

You have your past
And I have mine.
That can't be changed
As that is from another time.

Sometimes when we are together,
The thought does cross my mind
As to whether you are with me
Or if you're reliving that time.

I would often wonder,
If you were there with me
Or if I was merely a substitute
For a past memory.

Stepping Stones

Each experience we face
Is but a stepping stone,
For our destiny in life
Is not always known.

We have to accept our challenges
And rise to our defeats.
We find pleasure in our triumphs
As they prove that we aren't weak.

Our path in life
Is filled with stepping stones.
Each step leads us closer
So that our destiny is shown.

The loves of our past
Have taught us how to heal
When those loves subsided
And we learned that they weren't real.

As much pain as we've endured
From those memories of the past,
They were the stepping stones
That led us to our destiny at last.

Discovery

Thoughts of you are with me constantly.
I am powerless to the feelings you have uncovered.
You have awakened my heart and my eyes
With this great love that I have discovered.

You could never imagine all that I feel,
Nor could you fully understand all that I see
When I look into your eyes and see inside your soul.
I see your heart and feel the love you have for me.

I have stumbled across many fortunes in my travels
But the most rewarding of these has been your love.
It has brightened my heart and my life
And its depth compares to nothing above.

If my journey in life were to end at this moment
With my final days being spent with you,
Then I would perish having fulfilled my life's purpose
And that is to find the happiness that was long past due.

My New Awakening

My eyes have been opened
By your love ever so much.
My life has been greatly blessed
With your perfect and tender touch.

I'm experiencing things absent
From my life until now.
I don't know how I survived
But I managed somehow.

I'm seeing life with a new outlook.
I'm feeling true love deep within my soul.
And my heart is overflowing
With love that fills it whole.

I've been awakened to pure bliss
With warm sunshine all about.
I've been awakened to your love
That I hope never again to do without.

The splendor of your love and you
Is a constant blessing with me now.
This new awakening that I have
Has changed me for the better somehow.

I anticipate each tomorrow
With a sense of excitement and delight.
My new awakening is you.
Your love has granted me this sight.

My Mother's Eyes

In my mother's eyes
I can do no wrong
But little does she know
Her strength is my backbone.

My mother is soft and fragile
And so tender and sweet.
Her love is vast and overflowing
And she charms everyone that she meets.

Those who cross her path
Sense her love and devotion.
They see her good nature,
Her heart and her emotion.

In my mother's eyes
You see her endless love
For her family and children
That compares to nothing above.

Some other time
And in some other place
My mother's eyes would be just as loving
And they are the beauty of her face.

A Father's Love

There is no way to accurately describe
The love a father has for his child.
Words alone can not fully explain
The turmoil a man feels or his pain
When he is apart from his own,
A pain hidden and seldom shown.

A mother's love is usually more visually expressed
As the one who bore him and fed him from her breast.
A father's love is ever present as well
But it's not always easy for one to tell.
Fathers tend to keep their feelings inside
Which makes it difficult to see or even to describe.

You can see never-ending love in a mother's eye.
In a father's eye, you can see his strength and his pride.
A deeper look reveals his anguish and his pain
That mere words alone could never fully explain.
There is no way to accurately describe
The love a father has for his child.

God's Plan

I feel truly blessed at this moment
And it is all because of you.
You have changed my life for the better
Of that you have no clue.
With your presence, I've been graced,
And your sweet touch is the paste,
That holds my life in your hands
To do with as God plans.

In Body and In Soul

Mere words would not do justice
To express how much I care.
I feel so very close to you
And have much I want to share.

My life, my love, my heart,
Everything that makes me whole,
These things I want to share with you
In body and in soul.

Your presence in my life
Is truly a wonderful gift.
I've been so very blessed by you.
My spirit you've helped to lift.

I was granted sight
When blindness took its toll.
And I was led to you
In body and in soul.

A Risk Worth Taking

When we allow our hearts to feel
And we face life with an open mind,
The possibilities we have are endless.
Each relationship is one of a kind.

Some risks are worth taking,
Allowing yourself to care,
Experiencing the good things in life
And giving your heart to share.

Deciding when to go slow
Or when to open your heart and feel,
Living each day as a blessing,
Turning the fantasy into the real.

A risk worth taking
That is what you are to me,
A chance of something great
That can become reality.

I don't know how to act.
I'm not sure how to be.
But you are a risk worth taking,
At least you are to me.

If I Never Wake to See Tomorrow

If I never wake to see tomorrow,
I hope that you will know,
How deeply you have touched me,
And how vast my feelings flow.

Each day is a gift,
And uncertain as it is,
I don't want the chance to pass,
Or for my feelings to be amiss.

I've searched and searched,
In quiet and in peace,
For someone to love me,
To hold me while I sleep.

It was not expected.
It was a total surprise.
With a touch of your hand,
You opened my eyes.

I now see possibilities
Of greater things to pass.
You inspire much in me,
An inspiration I hope will last.

If I never see tomorrow,
I hope that you can see
How much better I am knowing you
And just how much you mean to me.

I've Been Made Whole

My feelings explode
In an indescribable way.
It's hard to put into words
All that those feelings say.

They abound without measure
When your soul reaches mine.
And they peak with the pleasure
When your heart touches mine.

It's not easy to explain
All that I feel deep inside.
It's more powerful than me,
Like the waves in the tide.

You've given me your everything,
Your body and your soul.
I am so blessed that you found me
And now I've been made whole.

I Loved You All Along

To be admired from a distance
For time so very long,
That is what you felt for me
And yet you held your tongue.

Patience is a virtue
And frustrating at its best.
Yet some things are worth the wait
And patience is worth the test.

The way you make me feel,
The special things you do,
The sweetest things you say
Make me fall more in love with you.

When you look into my eyes,
You see me in body and in soul.
You see beyond the outside.
You see all of me, my whole.

You and yours complete me.
My purpose in life is known.
Even before I found you,
I loved you all along.

Overwhelmed

I am completely overwhelmed
With life and with you.
Perhaps we could take a step back,
Slow down and take in the view.

I don't want to lose sight
Of what I feel inside,
But my emotions are peaked
And I want to run and hide.

The thought of the future
With you and with me
Has me over-burdened
And filled with excess worry.

I need to look before I jump.
I need to see before I begin to run.
I need to be certain what I do is right.
I need to be sure you are it for my life.

I am confused and in a daze,
Full of wonder and with doubt.
I am not sure anymore
If I am to be with you or without.

My heart is racing.
Each beat is quicker than the last.
I am in a struggle
With the future and the past.

It is too soon for me to know
If my decision is to be.
It is too soon for you to feel
This kind of love for me.

If you need perfection
Or something pretty in your life,
Perhaps you mistake that in me.
I may not be cut out to be your wife.

I am all mixed up inside.
My past haunts me like a ghost.
I turned away from a great love
When I thought that is what I needed most.

Then I turned to you
Whose love is even greater.
How can I be sure
That your love is my savior?

A sound decision
I can not make
Not at this time
Not in this place.

I am too overwhelmed within
And need time to think and learn.
I don't know what I feel anymore.
My heart is filled with pain and burn.

I am caught in the middle
Between greatness and splendor.
Do I choose love or does love choose me?
Do I walk away without knowing for sure?

Love is a power greater than all.
It motivates and devastates all in its path
With a ferocity without measure.
How do we survive the aftermath?

I am not sure that there is one love for me.
I am not sure that it is within my destiny
To find love and keep it forever and always
To be blessed and happy for all of my days.

I have my doubts you see
About a future for you and for me.
I am no longer sure
That we will endure.

I am confused within
And overwhelmed about
Whether you are it for me
And I have my doubts.

I feel as if I owe you
For spending time with me,
For all of the love you give
And your vast generosity.

I do have love for you
And love you with great passion.
I just don't know if it matches yours
In manner or in fashion.

I am afraid that I may settle
And live to regret the chance
Of no longer seeking love
Once you touched my hand.

I know that you will love me
Forever and for always.
I know that we will have a happy life
For all of our days.

What I don't know for sure
Is if I turned away from my destiny
When I turned to you.
How do I know you are it for me?

How can I be certain
That we will be happily ever after?
How will I know
That my days will be filled with laughter?

I am overwhelmed and confused
And my insides scream in pain.
I do not want anyone to hurt.
I do not want me to be the blame.

I am frightened and I am scared.
My future is approaching fast.
I don't know what I want.
The questions are too vast.

Seeing you is believing,
I guess that is what I could say.
Your touch makes my doubts subside.
It takes my breath away.

To close my eyes and think of you,
I feel your touch on my skin.
Each touch I feel from you is
Feeling love that will never end.

You are in my head
And you are in my heart.
I just don't want to make a mistake
At least not from the start.

We have time together
To learn and to grow.
Lets take this time together
So that we will know

That we were meant to be
Without a wonder or a doubt,
That we were meant to be
With each other and not without.

I love you in this moment.
And in this moment I must dwell.
If I look beyond this moment,
The doubts rise and swell.

I want to be loved
Of that there is no doubt.
But I also need to love
And that I can not do without.

To love and to be loved
Is what I seek the most in life,
Matched for feeling and emotion
In equality and in strife.

I am not sure I have that with you.
I have too many concerns and doubts.
I don't think I love you the same as you love me.
And that is something you should not do without.

I have love for you
But my heart is not yours alone.
I love another as well,
A love that has yet to be gone.

I come to you with a heavy heart.
It is weighed down with turmoil and inner fight.
If I turn away from you, I turn away from love.
But if I turn away from him, do I turn away from life?

I know you love me more.
I feel it in your touch.
I know I love you too
But what if it isn't enough?

What if I fail you in your quest for love?
What if I fail us in our quest for life?
With all of my confusions and overwhelming doubts,
Are you sure you want me to be your wife?

Honesty

Your touch compares to nothing
That I have ever felt before.
Alone with you I am blissful.
My feelings I can't ignore.

Yet my heart is not all yours.
I can no longer pretend that it is.
The person that you expect me to be
Is nothing more than what you wish.

I am not a dream come true,
As you so want me to be.
I am just plain and ordinary.
I am nothing more than me.

At times I see us together
Sharing our lives as one.
And other times I don't,
Our lives, yes, but not a home.

Excess is what we have.
You and me are fine.
But the extra lives involved
Are not something I want as mine.

The perfect life you envision
With my standing by your side
Is not something I see as real
Nor do I see myself as your bride.

The expectations that you have,
The things you need in your life,
Are not something I can own up to
Nor do I want to take that dive.

I would spiral downward
And perhaps never see the light
Until it was too late to render,
Too late to make it right.

You deserve much more
Than I could ever give you.
Don't waste your time on me
You will only end up blue.

I'm Merely Me

Does it make me horrible
To cast your love aside?
Am I blinded by worries
That I fail to take your side?

Does it make me horrible
To cast a guilty blame?
Am I so caught up with me
That I fail to see the shame?

Does it make me horrible
To cast your heart away?
Am I so self doubted
That I fail to see the way?

I'm not horrible.
I'm merely me,
So full of doubt
And filled with honesty.

Words that pain
And words that cut
Have led me discover,
I can't love enough.

I'm not horrible
Can't you see?
I'm merely human,
And treading selfishly.

My love for you
Has faded over time.
I'm not capable of love.
I can't lead you blind.

You deserve much more
Than I can ever give
And to find true happiness
In the life that you live.

I have locked my heart away
And shut its doors for now.
The key is frozen in ice and despair
And to not love again, I do vow.

I'm not horrible.
I'm merely me,
With very little hope
Of someone finding the key.

False Promises

I can give you the present
As I deal with my past,
But I can't promise you the future.
I can't promise this will last.

I have issues and I have pain.
My heart is not in one piece.
The best I can do, the most I can say
Is tell you my heart is on lease.

And short term at best,
I can't think too far ahead.
My pain however old is real.
Time is needed to get it out of my head.

I am confused and I am in pain
Each day that I live.
I've been mistreated and I've been hurt.
This makes it hard for me to give.

I don't want to give you false promises
Or a false sense of love.
I can give you friendship
That is all I know of.

In Time

Time will tell the reason.
Time will show the way,
Whether we were meant to love
Beyond this moment and this day.

I am incomplete
And have been for some time.
But I was whole for a while
When you were mine.

We were together
One in body and in soul.
Our hearts blended
And we were a whole.

Nothing is permanent,
Temporary at best,
We loved with great fury
But now we must rest.

Feelings set aside,
Memories in capacity of great,
Emotions on high,
The rest left to fate.

Time will tell the reason.
Time will show the way,
Whether we shall love again
Beyond tomorrow and today.

Man's Plan

It was God's plan in the beginning
For what we found with each other
To be together and be as one
To have each one and not another.

But time was the enemy
For what we found and lost.
A nightmare revealed,
God's plan was the cost.

What once you held in your hands
Has now gone astray.
You opened up your hands
And let me get away.

I Hurt, I Care, I Feel

You've shown me kindness
By just being you.
You're helping me see
What it is I need to do.

But what price do we pay
When we love within our sin?
Does it make us weak
Or stronger in the end?

I have undiscovered feelings
That I'm not allowed to show.
I care a little more each day
As our friendship improves and grows.

I value your wisdom,
Your strength and your heart.
I hold your friendship dear to me
And vow not to let life tear it apart.

You are my eyes
When blindness fails to let me see
The strength that I do have
That is deep within me.

The me that is there
But hidden from sight,
The me that I've lost,
Sheltered from the light.

How can I express
All that I feel?
How can I share with you
The nightmare that's been real?

I'm afraid to care,
To endure more pain
When my heart gets broken
As it has time and again.

Am I so unlovable
That no one takes a chance
To get to know me better
To take my hand and let me dance?

I hurt so much each day
But I am afraid to cry.
Crying shows my failure
So it's better if I lie

And pretend that I am fine
Without a care in the world.
But deep down inside,
I'm just a frightened little girl.

I hide all my bruises
From the world I do.
Many bruises I do have
And yet no one has a clue.

Some bruises never heal.
Some hurt is always there.
All of the pain that I have
Makes it hard for me to care.

I give of my body,
Not my heart nor my soul.
But I'm starting to have feelings
And that was not the goal.

I hurt, I care, I feel.
My eyes have begun to leak.
The pain is creeping out of me
To strengthen what is weak.

I expect the worst
And I guess I always will.
It's all I've ever known
And makes it easy not to feel.

You've helped me see
That my journey has an end.
You've led me to the light
And I need you as my friend.

I want you as a man
But I need you as a friend.
I have to release that pain in me
So my heart can finally mend.

Once mended if I choose
I can try to love again.
My heart will decide
The if, the where, the when.

I'm hanging onto so much.
I know I need not be
So intent to keep my pain
Deep inside of me.

If I let it go
A little at a time,
The pain will not overcome
And my heart can be all mine.

I hurt, I care, I feel
These that I've vowed not to do,
But as each day goes by,
I find that I do want to.

I want to love again
And to be loved in return.
Will the timing ever match
So that I can use all I've learned?

My past has gone away
To repeat never again.
I want to find love
But I'm not sure just when.

Once I've found me
And healed my heart and soul
Then I can love again
And make it worth the toll.

My Heart of Hearts

In my heart of hearts
And in my pain of pain
Just by knowing you
I'll never be the same.

You brought me kindness
Like a true friend should.
Your spirit is beautiful,
Your heart, kind and good.

You opened yourself to me
And allowed me a peek at your soul.
You showed me true friendship
And that I alone can be made whole.

The chance of knowing you
Is something I will ever cherish.
I wouldn't have missed it for anything.
Your friendship I hope will never perish.

I love the person you are inside.
A true friend you will always be,
A crutch, a shoulder, a confidant
With me in spirit to guide me.

But give me some time
For this break to mend.
And in the end I promise
I will be your friend.

I can't deny I wanted much more
Even though I knew the cost.
But don't worry or fret or fear,
Our friendship will not be lost.

I've only just found you.
I'll not let you go.
My life needs you in it
And I need you so.

I just wanted to be held
By you for a while.
A comfort I needed.
You make me smile.

I do hurt right now
This pain inside
In my heart of hearts
I do confide.

Just don't lose me
In all of this mess.
Keep me close okay
'Cause this is just a test.

A test of endurance
For friends that we are
To test our ability
To rise and go far.

I am truly sorry
That I allowed myself to feel,
But it just felt so good,
So right and so real.

I do need you right now
To make this pain go away
And I need you tomorrow
And each and every day.

You got it all wrong
When you said I would take
What I wanted and needed
And then take my break.

I saw great potential
In you and in me.
I saw something spectacular
That you failed to see.

I didn't want forever
Or even a year.
I just wanted you
In the now and the here.

In my heart of hearts
In a shield of concrete,
You broke through the solid
And you made me weep.

With you I had feelings
That haven't been felt.
Many years and longer
Without feelings I dealt.

I've lived and I've learned
One day at a time.
Now I have to accept
With reason or rhyme

That you felt nothing for me,
No feelings returned.
I will be okay in time,
Another pain I've earned.

I care so much it hurts
In my heart of hearts.
I will one day find
The whole to my parts.

Your concern and your worry
Need not be.
I'll rise above.
I'll make you see.

I can't be mean to you
As much as I'd like,
But I do plan to show you,
You're wrong and I'm right.

In my heart of hearts
I see you there,
Through the pain and the hurt
And I know you care.

My Torment

I yearn for the best
While expecting the worst.
My head is in the clouds
But my feet are firm in the dirt.

I lead with my heart
And not with my head,
So I've been told,
So it's been said.

I've tormented you
While tormenting myself.
To escape my feelings I can not do.
I can not disguise what was felt.

I haven't any regrets
Nor do I have a guilty mind.
The opportunity to know you
Has let a friendship bind.

Bound by ties, strong and firm,
Their strength will keep me true,
True to my heart and to me.
A strength up until now seen only by few.

Why does it hurt so bad to care?
Why does it hurt so bad to feel?
My feelings were not false.
I felt not fantasy but real.

I mourn for all that is lost
And what may now never be.
My eyes were not blinded
Just shielded temporarily.

Shielded from the truth
Of what I need to find,
Shielded from the lies
That formed in my mind.

From years and years of pain
Of darkness seeking light,
From years and years of hurt
And accepting the wrongs as if they were right.

I am worth so much more
Than I allow myself to be.
So much has been buried
Deep inside of me.

Layer after layer
Of pain and hurt and fear,
Uncovered, little by little
With each cry of a tear.

My torment is alive
With each minute that does pass.
I do have inner faith
That my torment will not last.

That it will not last for long,
When I find what I do seek,
I seek to find me
And be awakened from my sleep.

My soul has rested long
And my body is so tired,
Tired from barely living
And from barely getting by.

My torment is my own.
My hurt and pain, I've caused.
I know what I must do,
To find the me that I have lost.

My task at hand is known.
The choices I must make.
I must choose to find me.
This is the path I must take.

I have to be alone,
Not the half of a pair.
I have to be alone,
A task surely hard to bear.

I have so much love to share.
There is so much love inside of me.
The key to share my love
Is to first find me.

No Words

The words flow so easily
When I sit and write.
I am so filled with hurt,
Inner turmoil and fright.

I fear of abandonment
And longing for you.
I fear I will have lost you
When this journey is through.

Of little faith, that I am,
With sadness and worry,
I take each day with caution
And am afraid just to be.

My words help to heal
All that I've known.
My words help me deal
With what I've been shown.

My eyes have been opened
And made so aware,
That my life as it was
To me was not fair.

More deserving I am,
In being happy and free,
I deserve to be loved
And for love to find me.

My words help to soothe
The pain that has been caused
In a life filled with fear
And my security lost.

My sense of self worth
Was lost along the way.
My own independence
Was the price I did pay.

For years of pure pain
Suffering and hell,
A hurt so deep
That makes me unwell.

Not fit to be loved
Cared for or needed,
Not fit to be wanted
But instead mistreated.

A life without love
I know all too well,
A life with much pain
Explained in detail.

I need to be loved
Cared for and needed.
I want to be loved
And never mistreated.

No words, no words
Could ever explain
What I endured,
My hurt and my pain.

My words do haunt me
And so does my past,
But I have to overcome,
I have to outlast.

I have to rise up
Above the hurt and the pain.
I have to overcome.
I have much to gain.

I can't ignore you
As my words you are in.
I can't look away.
I just can't pretend.

Much meaning there was
And my heart it did feel.
There were feelings for you
Not pretend, they were real.

Imbedded in my words
Between the worry and doubt,
You'll find love there for you
That I can't do without.

A need that I have
Down deep within
A love that is there
To be claimed again.

It is all up to you
As to what we become.
You possess all the power.
It beats to your drum.

My words are my own
But I share them with you.
But words not alone
Can make me seem true.

You have to see that yourself
With your own eyes you do.
You have to see that I care
And have a great desire for you.

But it's far deeper than that,
More than words could explain.
You have a hold on me,
My heart, soul and brain.

A need and a want
All set together,
A need and a want
That I hope to tire never.

No words, no words
Lets vow just to see.
Let feelings take hold
And see what is to be.

Take a chance at love,
At knowing love with me.
Give me a chance.
Take a chance and see.

Don't give up the fight
Or run away and flee.
Run to the feeling.
Please, run to me.

You Instead Hurt Me

What we had was less than innocent.
We took a chance with a love affair.
What was not supposed to be serious
Was filled instead with warmth and care.

We fell before we knew it,
Me first, as time did tell.
My feelings were quite evident
Hammered in my heart like a nail.

A spell you did cast over me
And love that I did feel.
What started out as innocent
Ended with a hand that fate did deal.

A fear that you did have
That I would one day go,
Once I no longer needed you.
You failed to let me show.

To prove to you my passion,
To heal my hurt and pain,
To fill you with my love inside,
A love that would surely reign.

To reign above all others
In depth and lasting power,
Forever to be remembered,
For each minute of each hour.

For time we had so little
And quickly you did flee.
Something did come over you.
You felt something strong for me.

You chose instead to turn,
To turn away and leave.
You left me all alone
To find myself in me.

Now pain and hurt I have
Filling me with fear.
What little hope is fading.
The pain is like a spear.

Cutting into my heart
And hurting oh so bad,
The pain I feel for you
Is like nothing I've ever had.

Pain and I were friends
And hurt I knew so well
Until I did meet you
And fell under your spell.

You want to be my friend
And I want so much to be
A friend to you forever
But we have to wait and see.

To see if you will stay
In my life for all of time,
To see if you will be there
When the me I do find.

In the end to sum up
All that has come to be,
So that you would not hurt,
You instead hurt me.

Abandoned Feelings

My feelings you abandoned.
Their worth not shown.
No credit was given
For a future unknown.

A peak was never reached,
Perfection never met.
You chose to abandon
What was never fully set.

The potential was there,
A foundation set in stone.
A great friendship was formed
But now I'm all alone.

Alone to sit and ponder,
My life its ups and downs,
My past to be revisited.
My smiles have turned to frowns.

More meaning was in my heart.
More depth was in my soul.
You reached a place in me
And now my heart must pay the toll.

The price of feelings buried
Locked away and lost,
The hurt is all too vibrant.
My pain is now the cost.

I've failed at love before.
This time is not the first.
Of love that did fail me,
This one is by far the worst.

My feelings have been abandoned.
The pain inside does hurt.
I was left in mid emotion.
With disaster we did flirt.

There is no blame to cast
For my hurt and misery.
I should have known better
Than to fall in love with thee.

Intentions whether good
Sometimes result in feeling bad.
The feelings there were for you
Were stronger than I'd ever had.

This is not to be taken lightly.
Tread softly and with care,
One day I hope you realize
The great potential that was there.

My feelings were abandoned.
My heart and soul you've seen.
More knowledge you do know.
Please don't abandon me.

No Escape

I have tried to fight it.
I have tried not to feel.
I try to hide the pain
But it is still so real.

I can not escape thoughts of you.
You are with me always it seems,
During each of my waking hours
And each night, you invade my dreams.

I am stuck in this rut.
I can't seem to crest this bump.
My heart was not supposed to feel.
Now, it can barely manage a thump.

I can not escape you.
I tried to flee.
I turned and ran.
I can not escape me.

I confided in you.
I gave more than I should.
I gave more than I had
And all that I could.

This was not supposed to end this way.
It still seems so wrong to me.
How do I shed these feelings?
Do I hide them or let them be?

I can not escape my pain.
I can not escape this hurt.
My wants and needs aside,
The pain only gets worse.

I hurt all over,
Deep down inside.
I'm haunted by you.
I've been cast aside.

There is no escape.
There is no way out.
My pain is apart of me.
It's what I am all about.

Nothing was intended,
Coincidence not fault.
My feelings were valued
Like a grain of salt.

I can't fully comprehend
All that came to be.
My wounds are still very fresh
So it is too soon for me.

I can't let go.
It still feels so strong.
There is no escape,
No right and no wrong.

I get sad at times
For what might have been.
I'm selfish I know
And I'm losing a friend.

I can't escape you.
You will ever be
A part of my heart
And a part of me.

Resurrection

My heart still aches for you
With each day I face anew.
And with every breath I take,
My heart continues to break.

I felt when I didn't think I could feel.
And those feelings for you are with me still.
They cause me grief and they cause me pain.
These feelings for you will always remain.

I had no pretense of falling for you.
It came completely out of the blue.
I was caught off guard and I was unprepared.
My heart and soul were completely bared.

They were unprotected and in full view.
Much like on a platter, they were offered to you.
You declined the offer and cast them away.
The pain that remains is your debt to pay.

I will always hold dear your memory to me.
It will not shield the light for me to see.
I thought the pain would subside and disappear,
But the pain is with me now and here.

I barely had time to blink or catch my breath.
And then my feelings were sentenced to their death.
I loved and I lost, that's nothing new.
And now I'm left to pretend I don't want you.

It hurts to think what might have been.
It's much better for us to merely pretend
That it was just a big mistake
And what was felt was fake.

It was real to me, very real indeed,
So much so it's taken residence within me.
I loved and I felt and for you, I so cared.
This pain is not something that can be spared.

In time my wounds will eventually heal,
But not what's in me, not what I feel.
Love with no depth and no direction
Certainly deserves some sort of resurrection.

You are so alive in my soul and in my heart.
I can't seem to grasp why we are apart.
I'm here for you, for now and ever.
It's your choice to make if it becomes never.

My Bitter Confession

Life has led me to this confusion
Of knowing wrong from right.
Life has given me this choice
And put it plain in sight.

I just want you to know what I am feeling.
It is the only thing for certain that I do know.
It was so very easy for me to develop these feelings for you,
And it is so very hard for me to let them go.

I love you, plain and simple.
And I mean all that's been said.
Whether acted upon or not,
You're in my heart, you're in my head.

Wherever life may take you,
Through times of good and bad,
Take this knowledge with you.
Recall the happy and the sad.

And although I do hope and wish and want
For the timing to be right.
I will do better to shelter my hurt
And keep it hidden from full sight.

Some moments are worse than others.
The hurt sometimes takes flight,
Like when I am at my weakest,
When I am compelled to write.

And I am completely powerless
Against what flows to paper from pen.
My words can be so very vivid and real
As I experience the hurt all over again.

And because you shared so much of you with me,
You feel what I feel when you read my thoughts.
You are as powerless as I against my words,
But as you read them, you forgive my faults.

I loved you in secrecy.
I loved you in despair.
I was afraid to admit,
To disclose, to bare.

To confess our sins
And tell our tales,
Each life is a story
Full of triumphs and fails.

As bitter as it is to hurt,
As sad as it is to lose,
I chanced it all with you
And again I would so choose.

As I Pass Through Each Day

I'm all out of words.
There is nothing left to say.
My voice goes unheard
As I pass through each day.

My heart is so heavy.
The pressure is there,
Full of love without reason
But not meant to share.

My prayers are unanswered.
My wants left astray.
No guidance is before me
As I pass through each day.

My hurt now rules me,
No struggle, no plea.
My heart just longs
To be set free.

Free from the pain,
Its ache to go away.
Free from this love
As I pass through each day.

I Want

I want to give all of myself
To just be free and let me be.
I want to show you and know you.
I want you to see all of me.

But I am afraid,
Overflowing with great fear,
Afraid to lose at love again,
Afraid you won't be here.

When I open my eyes
You may be gone,
Like the end of the night
Once the light is shown.

And then the light will fade
When the day comes to an end
And then darkness will come
And the night will begin again.

I want you to know
All the sides there are to me.
I want to be able to open myself to you.
I want to come to you completely free.

I want you to feel
All that I have in me to give.
I want you with me
In the life that I live.

I can't explain,
Nor can I understand
Why I seek more with you
And without a plan.

When I look at you
I see far deeper than I should.
I see much more than I deserve
And hope for something beyond good.

I want you to have all of me.
I want to give myself to you,
Something to always be cherished
And shared with very few.

The Clock

The minutes tick slowly,
Each hour an eternity,
As I wait for a voice that's never heard
And the despair screams from within me.

Neglected and unwanted
That is how I feel right now.
Circumstances as they are,
Time fades with each passing hour.

I ask for very little.
My demands are few.
I just need your touch
And to spend a little time with you.

Tell me about your day
And your plans to come.
Tell me about your night.
Lets watch the setting sun.

How desperate I must be
To watch a ticking clock,
Not knowing what you feel,
Unsure even of your thoughts.

Reach out and grab me.
Don't let me get away.
I'm yours if you'll have me.
Please want me I pray.

Potential for Satisfaction

You are destined to die
Alone and in pain
Surrounded by your inner demons
That will pour down like rain.

You are stubborn and harsh,
Unyielding of your love.
Tread softly I beg.
Look within yourself and above.

You are better than this.
You deserve so much more,
As do us all,
But you choose to ignore.

Satisfaction is within your reach
But you have failed to see
Everything that you could possibly want
Is all embodied in me.

Don't give in or concede.
The foundation is set.
Build on what we've started.
I won't give up on you yet.

The potential is there.
I see it in your eyes.
I'll not admit to defeat.
I've already forgiven your lies.

The Drunk

Surrounded by beer cans
On a heap in the floor,
That is where I will find him
When I walk through the door.

This is the future I see.
He is messed up and dazed.
And when he gets drunk,
He becomes somewhat crazed.

What pain does he hide
When he sits and he drinks?
What does this solve?
What should I think?

I think he is scared
From the pain he has had.
He is afraid to give
And that is really quite sad.

He limits his options
When he closes off himself
From feelings and emotions
That he won't allow be felt.

He is destined to live
Alone and in pain.
He is destined to die
Pretty much the same.

The Puppet Master

Neither your lies nor your harshness
Can keep me away.
I return again and again
And you know I won't stray
Far from your presence
For more than a day.

You keep me so close
And wound so tight.
Around your finger I am,
And I know that isn't right.
But I return again anyway
Without effort or fight.

You control this relationship.
I play by your rule.
I am someone I'm not.
I play the part of your fool.
You keep me at hand
And can be ever so cruel.

I've lost sight of me.
I've taken on a new role.
I play the part falsely
And it's taking its toll.
The real me is lost.
You have all the control.

If you only knew
What you hold in your hand.
If you would look deep
And could just understand.
My eyes have the answers.
My heart is in demand.

You've landed a beauty
Of that you can see.
But the beauty is within
Far deep and beneath,
Locked away and hidden
For those who possess the key.

Two Roses

One Rose of red
Out of a life so blue,
One Rose of yellow
Out of a fondness for you.

My life was empty.
My life was untrue.
My life is now filled
With a desire for you.

My heart is guarded,
Shielded with concrete.
But your bright green eyes,
They will be its defeat.

You are my weakness.
You always will be.
One Rose for you,
One Rose for me.

An Ode to the Old Man

I lack the strength to set you free.
My greatest weakness
You will always be.

I lack the courage to be alone.
I am too timid
To run away and go home.

I lack the will power to do what is right.
My one true want and desire
Is to have you in my sight.

I lack the faith to be true to me.
You are my other half, my soul mate,
But it just can't be.

The Roses Are No Longer in Bloom

I was not enough for you then.
I am too much for you now.
Our dreams and desires will never reach one destination.
There is no future for you and me.

Our paths crossed once, but the timing was less than ideal.
Our paths crossed again, but we had changed, our lives were
different.
Our paths will continue to cross as time endures,
But we aren't meant to find happiness together.

You live in your reality, and I live in mine.
We aren't willing to exchange ourselves or our lives for each
other.
I have the security that I need,
And in return, I must set you free.

My heart breaks each time I think about what might have been.
But for you and me, the Roses have died and the petals are
scattered.
But the mark of the Roses will always be evident in me,
And in the love that our hearts found that is ever after shattered
Because we were meant to be, but not in this time.

May we meet again in another time and another place
When the Roses are again in bloom
And may we gather the petals that were scattered
And reunite what should have been, but was not.

Until You

Until you found me
My life was so blue.
I was content, but not happy
Until I found you.

Until you found me
My smiles were few.
My spirit had died
Until I found you.

Until you found me
I never really knew
What I was missing
Until I found you.

Until you found me
A lasting love I was due.
My heart had no owner
Until I found you.

Until you found me
My heart was torn in two
With only love for my children
Until I found you.

Until you found me
I was half, not whole
My life was not complete
Until I found your soul.

Heart and Soul

My heart is in your hands.
Our love is still yet new.
My feelings for you run deep
And are absolutely true.

You appeared out of nowhere
And entered into my life.
You've left me yearning for you
And wanting to be your wife.

My heart has been shielded
For time so very long,
But you have conquered and disarmed it
And left me with feelings very strong.

I had given up on love
And let myself be defeated,
Until you came and rescued me
And showed me all love was not depleted.

I have found love with you
And you have made me whole.
Your love and you complete me.
You have me, heart and soul.

Forever and A Day

I have truly been blessed
With this gift of love from you.
You have brightened my world
With your goodness and virtue.

You are a dream come true.
A more perfect man I could never find.
You are absolutely amazing.
You are wonderful, rare, one of a kind.

You have blessed my life with love
And touched my heart so tenderly.
When I thought it was not possible,
You fell in love with me.

My heart is in your hands
And it is yours to mold.
My life is now with you
Until we are gray and old.

I will love you forever
Forever and a day.
I am yours for always
And always I will stay.

I need you in my life
In my life forevermore
And with our hearts together
Our love will always soar.

Once In A Lifetime

Once in a lifetime
Cupid finds his mark.
Love is started
With one small spark.

A friendship forms,
Meaningful and true,
And then it deepens
With feelings so new.

One little spark
Ignited by one small touch
Becomes a deep emotion
That means so much.

There is no reason
Nor is there any rhyme,
True love will develop
All within due time.

When least expected
Love finds its way,
Once in a lifetime,
One glorious day.

With and Without

I have had so much pain in my life.
Misery and unhappiness have ruled me.
I have been without love for so very long.
With you, I have realized what love could be.

You have changed my life for better
And blessed me in so many ways.
I am truly consumed by what I feel
And look forward to loving you always.

I can see forever with you.
My spirit has been lifted so high.
My days have meaning and purpose.
Without you, how did I ever survive?

It is said that you don't know
What you have until it is gone.
I have seen what I have missed
And lived without for so long.

I never expected to find love
Or to feel the way I do.
But I know without a doubt
That I have love for you.

Two Hearts

Two hearts together
One beat at a time
One life together
In perfect rhyme.

One love discovered
True and strong
Two hearts together
For time so long.

Each day together
From dusk to dawn
Two hearts forever
Beating as one.

My love for you
Perfect and true
My heart is yours
It belongs to you.

Two hearts together
Beating in rhyme
Two hearts forever
'Til the end of time.

To Feel My Love

It pains me greatly to know
That you aren't feeling my love.
I truly do love you deeply and madly
With more passion than you could dream of.

I don't have a thought that excludes you.
You are my life and my every breath.
You are my present and my future.
My love for you has no measure or depth.

Thoughts of you greet me each morning
And your smile guides me through each day.
I am comforted in sleep knowing you exist.
I thank God for you each night when I pray.

You are my lifeline and my world
And I treasure each moment with you.
My love for you is without end.
When we are apart, my heart is blue.

The essence of you
Is the foundation of me.
To feel my love,
You merely have to be.

A Song of Woe

Where did I go wrong?
Have your feelings for me changed?
Like a truly sad, sad song,
My heart is greatly pained.

I can't figure you out.
I can't see into your heart.
I can't tell what you are about.
I fear that we will part.

My heart sings a song of woe,
For a love so strong and right.
My love weeps softly so,
Its tears hidden from sight.

Where did I go wrong?
Did I fail our love in some way?
Will this pain endure for long?
I can't stand it even for one day.

A Destiny Foretold

I am very insecure
Of how you feel for me.
Your ways are set and firm.
Relax and let it be.

Let it be fulfilled
And what we've found will grow.
What life holds for us
Living will let us know.

Our destinies were formed
Long before things came our way.
We choose our paths to follow.
The pieces will fall as they may.

What was meant to be will happen.
Good things come to those who wait.
A life of uncertainty and patience
Is far better than one with no love and hate.

Our paths crossed for a reason.
We were meant to be somehow.
We need to rise to the challenge,
Build on what we feel right now.

My feelings are still growing.
For you my love is vast.
With trepidation I look to the future
And must look away from my past.

A past so full of lessons
With times of sorrow and of pain,
But with its own blessings,
Its wisdom I seek to gain.

Bad times that do not break us
Only serve to make us strong.
The lessons that they teach us
Show us right from wrong.

To be fulfilled in life
Means to take a chance or two.
And there is nothing that I'd rather
Than to spend my life with you.

I don't have all the answers
Or know what tomorrow holds.
I do know that I love you,
A destiny foretold.

The Still of Time

The still of time is lingering by.
The missing of you is killing inside.
The pain of love is hurting my
Heart.

The hurt of care is paining a cry.
The loving of you is sighing a high.
The still of time is hurting my
Body.

The tear of a cry is within my eye.
The drop of a tear is rolling by.
The cry of love is hurting my
Soul.

The empty of love is but a sigh.
The lonely of heart is all but a cry.
The still of time is hurting my
Love.

The Heart, It Hurts

The pain is unbearable.
The hurt is worse.
The love is strengthened.
The heart, it hurts.
The tears are falling.
The cries are loud.
The eyes are swelling.
The soul is proud.
The body is breaking.
The limbs are weak.
The organs are draining.
The bones, they creak.
The pain is unbearable.
The hurt is worse.
The love is strengthened.
The heart, it hurts.

My Perfect Love

Life blessed me with
My own perfect love.
It's like a dream come true
From the sky above.
I wished and I dreamed
For my perfect guy.
Life came through for me
And sent you from the sky.
From the bottom of my heart,
I truly grew to care.
From the depth of my soul,
I realized all I could share.
All my prayers were answered,
Mostly by fate.
Now I have my perfect love,
My perfect mate.
I never knew life could be
So perfect and fine.
Now I know it can,
Now that you're mine.
Like the miracle and perfection
Of the serenity of a dove,
I searched and finally found
My perfect love.

Perfect Images

I followed you blindly throughout all of time.
I saw nothing of your weaknesses or imperfections.
I'd found my perfect love.
Blindly I walked down life's path
With the golden sunshine all about.
All was perfect.
Life was perfect.
All these images were perfect to me.
These perfect images of you and me,
Love, happiness and the future,
Then reality struck little by little.
My perfect images became blemished.
My perfect world began to fall apart.
The person I was began to fade.
I'd changed since we met.
Our love became cloudy and we began to drift.
We began to fade
And I began to fall.
I lost my hold on my life.
The thought of all that was perfect ending, took control.
I almost lost me.
Little by little, I've slowly pieced my world back together.
It is not in reality perfect,
But in my mind,
All my images of you and of life
Are perfect images.

Your Lingering Goodbye

As the sweet goodbye of you lingers in my mind,
I sit and reminisce about my past,
And hope and wonder if in my future you will be there.
Each time we depart, I feel as if it's for forever.
I feel as if you are not coming back.
I keep remembering your goodbye and
The lingering haunts me.
Your goodbye is no different from times before.
There is an emptiness in my heart as you go.
I am so secure in myself when I am by your side.
The security dissolves as you leave.
As your loving goodbye lingers in my mind,
I find myself missing you
And hope and wonder if you will always be there for me.
Even though you have reassured me over and over again
That you will never leave me,
I still am uncertain as to whether or not
You will be there always.
Your goodbye remains behind as you slowly walk away
And I pray that in time you do return to my side
Where you will always stay.

I Miss You, A Memory, A Lost Love

I miss what we used to have.
I miss our love, how it was in the beginning
When we couldn't wait to see each other.
I miss you holding me in your arms and kissing me.
I miss you telling me that you love me.
I miss the beating of my heart as its pace raced
Whenever I heard your voice or saw your face.
I miss the smiles you put on my face
And the joy and love you put in my heart.
I miss the memories.
I miss the freshness of our love.
I miss you.
I miss a memory-a memory of a perfect love,
A memory of fantasy of eternal bliss.
I miss the anticipation and the excitement.
I miss the true feeling of being in love and being loved.
I miss love.
I miss your love.
It's so far hidden somewhere.
I can't find it.
It's lost.
I miss a lost love.
I miss our love.
I miss you.

The Autumn of Life

Have you ever wondered just what life was all about?
Have you ever wondered just what your purpose in it was?
Have you ever passed by a stream of water or a field of daisies?
Have you ever just inhaled all of life and its wonders?
Or have you just wandered aimlessly-missing so many wonders and delights?
The smell of autumn in the air, leaves and acorns on the ground,
The breeze with that slight nip as a chill passes through you,
Dew on the grass and in the trees, the fading sound of swings
And children playing.
Fading laughter, fading tears, an end and a beginning all at once,
Life is a wonder at all.
Changing seasons-a sign of continued life,
Babies-learning, exploring, experiencing
Life-season by season.

These Children of Mine

There was a little girl
Who had a headful of hair
With big bright brilliant marbled blue eyes
And skin so perfect and light.
She was so unlike her older brother
Who had eyes as dark as the night
With skin so handsome and tanned.
And as a baby, his head so bare and bald.

As different as night and day
Yet siblings just the same,
One brother, one sister, united by name.
Separated by years nearly of five,
Destined to grow and learn together.
Experiencing good times and bad,
Sharing life as friends and enemies,
To protect and be loyal
And sometimes to fight and disagree.
Planned-to enjoy years of laughter,
Love, devotion, friendship and harmony.
Loved-equally and endlessly
For all of time.

My Insecurity

My insecurity always seems
To follow me where I may go.
When first I met you,
My insecurity was there
Disguised as fear.
When first I began to love you,
My insecurity was there,
Disguised as uncertainty.
Now that I have fallen in love with you,
My insecurity has slowly faded away.
But every now and then,
I put pencil to paper
And my insecurity flows out in words.

The Poems That Never Were

He was the enemy
Yet she shared his name.
She played the victim
To the rules of his game.

She suppressed her emotions
And kept her thoughts in her head.
She left herself behind
And was his fool instead.

The words never came.
They remained hidden from sight.
The poems that never were
For so long were bottled up tight.

Those painful and revealing words
Were buried deeply over time.
She was afraid to expose them.
They remained in her sublime.

She accepted her life as it was
And had become someone she was not.
She was a stranger even to herself
And her inner self was left to rot.

The poems that never were
And the words that remained unsaid
Left her heart in pain
And filled her life with dread.

She was afraid to write
Or even utter what she thought.
Her mind was not her own.
He controlled her and they fought.

She was beaten down
Time and time again.
He was never her protector
Or even her friend.

She was treated like a consolation prize
Not like a woman that he loved.
She was never cared for or adored.
To the side she was always shoved.

The poems that never were
Are being written in this time
For she has found the strength she needed
To reveal the thoughts in her mind.

She settled for hell
Instead of reaching for the stars.
The many years she suffered
Have left many unhealed scars.

She learned a lot
And endured much pain
But she has risen above
And no longer plays his game.

The words were not spoken.
The thoughts were only for her.
Many great works left unwritten,
The poems that never were.

My Journey

I have traveled far and wide
To reach my life's destination.
I've traveled through my journey in life
With strength, fear and trepidation.

So many paths I've taken
To reach my place in the sun.
I've grown through the years
And many battles I have won.

Many mistakes have been made
In my quest for happiness.
These mistakes helped guide me
And can't be ignored nevertheless.

The love I have for my children
Is the greatest blessing I have known.
They are the miracles of my life,
No truer love could be shown.

My journey through life has led me
To this destination at last,
In which I can share with others
The crossings of my past.

The words of my life have been revealed
And my fairy tale ending has been found.
My words from the past whisper softly
With but a hint of a distant sound.

Many triumphs and defeats I've had
In life's roads, its curves and bends.
Happiness I've finally found
As my journey comes to this end.